CONTENT

Introduction...1

Maximum Weight Loss With 800 Calories.......................2

Getting Started 4

Diet Tips 5

Breakfast, Lunch & Dinner

Vegetarian Recipes Under 100 Calories

Carrot & Apple Smoothie 8

Creamy Red Pepper Soup...9

Tomato & Basil Soup...10

Creamy Tomato & Pesto Soup 11

Garlic Mushroom Wraps..12

Rosemary & Garlic Kale Chips 13

Cauliflower Rice...14

Vegetarian Recipes Under 200 Calories

Pink Grapefruit & Carrot Smoothie 16

Summer Berry Smoothie..17

Creamy Strawberry & Cherry Smoothie 18

Carrot & Ginger Smoothie 19

Homemade Hummus & Celery 20

Carrot, Coriander & Butterbean Soup...........................21

Cream Of Mushroom Soup...22

Avocado & Coriander (Cilantro) Soup 23

Asparagus Soup...24

Slow Cooked Tomato & Butterbean Soup......................25

Mozzarella Slices 26

Tomato & Olive Salad 27

Mediterranean Fried 'Rice' 28

Baked Eggs & Peppers 29

Poached Eggs & Rocket (Arugula)...................................30

Cheesy Baked Eggs 31

Roast Courgettes & Olives..32

Mushroom Courgetti...33

Slow Cooked Citrus Squash 34

Roast Pepper & Feta Salad 35

Slow Cooked Autumn Vegetable Casserole 36

Pizza Kale Chips 37

Mozzarella Chicory Boats 38

Cannellini Stuffed Peppers 39

Pomegranate Guacamole 40

Vegetarian Recipes Under 300 Calories

Pineapple & Avocado Smoothie...42

Raspberry Yogurt Smoothie 43

Quinoa & Berry Porridge 44

Apple Soufflé Omelette 45

Easy Banana Pancakes 46

Fresh Herb Scramble 47

Mozzarella & Tomato Mug Omelette 48

Herby Goat's Cheese Mug Omelette 49

Tomato & Basil Eggs 50

Cheese & Tomato Mini Cauliflower Pizzas........................51

Mediterranean Vegetable Bake...52

Bean & Quinoa Casserole..53

Courgette Fritters..54

Aubergine Fries...55

Egg & Lentil Salad..56

Mixed Bean Salad...57

Mozzarella Roast Vegetables 58

Halloumi & Asparagus Salad 59

Vegetable & Chickpea Casserole 60

Lentil & Sweet Potato Soup..61

Tomato & Fennel Gratin 62

Courgette 'Spaghetti' Pesto & Avocado Dressing.....................63

Avocado & Orange Salad 64

Greek Salad..65

Vegetarian Recipes Under 400 Calories

Creamy Lime & Mint Smoothie...68

Olive, Tomato & Herb Frittata 69

Avocado & Cheese Omelette..70

Chilli Mushroom & Bean Omelette 71

Cheese & Courgette Omelette 72

Halloumi Skewers 73

Low Carb Vegetable Lasagne 74

Avocado & Black-Eyed Pea Salad 75

Vegetarian Breakfast Casserole 76

Feta & Spinach Slice..77

Herby Tomato, Cannellini & Feta Salad................................78

Mozzarella & Aubergine Rolls 79

Italian Lentil Salad 80

Avocado & Beetroot Salad 81

Greek Style Salad...82

Tomato, Feta & Pomegranate Bake 83

Halloumi & Vegetable Traybake...84

Roast Balsamic Vegetables 85

Smokey Bean & Mushroom Stew..86

Spicy Bean Bake 87

Desserts

Recipes Under 230 Calories

Raspberry & Pistachio Fool 90

Chocolate Truffles 91

Nutty Chocolate Treats 92

Berry Compote & Vanilla Yogurt...93

Tropical Skewers & Fruit Sauce 94

Spiced Poached Pears..95

Raspberry Cupcakes..96

Quick Start Guides

The Essential
800 CALORIE
VEGETARIAN
Cookbook

A Quick Start Guide To Weight Loss With Intermittent Fasting And Mediterranean Diet Benefits.

Calorie Counted Vegetarian Recipe Book

First published in 2019 by Erin Rose Publishing

Text and illustration copyright © 2019 Erin Rose Publishing

Design: Julie Anson

ISBN: 978-1-9161523-1-1

A CIP record for this book is available from the British Library.

DISCLAIMER: This book is for informational purposes only and not intended as a substitute for the medical advice, diagnosis or treatment of a physician or qualified healthcare provider. The reader should consult a physician before undertaking a new health care regime and in all matters relating to his/her health, and particularly with respect to any symptoms that may require diagnosis or medical attention.

While every care has been taken in compiling the recipes for this Book we cannot accept responsibility for any problems which arise as a result of preparing one of the recipes. The author and publisher disclaim responsibility for any adverse effects that may arise from the use or application of the recipes in this book. Some of the recipes in this book include nuts. If you have a nut allergy it's important to avoid these.

INTRODUCTION

This easy-to-use vegetarian cookbook combines a low calorie, Mediterranean diet with intermittent fasting (IF) for quick and healthy weight loss.

This book provides you with weight loss tips, delicious recipes and all the essentials to make losing weight easier. You can decide how much weight you want to lose and adjust your diet to suit your lifestyle.

The benefits of the Mediterranean Diet have been endorsed by nutritionists and it's known to have significant health benefits such as reducing cholesterol, improving longevity, blood pressure, reducing the risk of heart disease, strokes, improving blood sugar levels and inflammation.

The latest research shows the optimum number of calories you can consume daily and still lose weight is 800 per day. Intermittent fasting on the 5:2 diet has been the secret of success for many peoples weight loss by restricting their calorie intake 2 days a week. Team that with the health benefits of Mediterranean style food and achieve great results!

This recipe book is an ideal place to start. It provides you with clear, concise information on how to get start losing weight and boosting your health. This book contains great-tasting, vegetarian, calorie-counted recipes which your taste buds and waist line will love!

Maximum Weight Loss With 800 Calories

A study by Oxford University showed an improvement in metabolism and cardiovascular health with an average 10kg weight loss in a group who restricted their calorie intake to 800 calories per day. This is around a third of the amount required to maintain weight, which for a man is 2,500 calories and less than half that recommended for a woman, which is 2,000 calories.

In addition, Newcastle University published a study which found that overweight type 2 diabetics who followed an 800-calorie-a-day diet for 12 weeks 'reversed' their diabetes plus they achieved and sustained average weight loss of 10kg.

Such calorie restriction is safe and doable for most people. Contrary to popular belief, fast weight loss can be maintained and it can help to lower blood sugar levels, in some cases even reversing pre-diabetes and type 2 diabetes.

So to maximise effective weight loss, you can restrict your daily calorie intake to 800 calories a day for up to 12 weeks. Or you can restrict calories for just 2 days a week, as in the 5:2 diet plan and eat normally on the other 5 days.

Another popular and proven successful weight loss technique is Time Restricted Eating (TRE). Basically this means eating all calories within a certain time frame each day. Often this can be a window of 8 to 16 hours a day, stretching the overnight fasting period, so you would consume no calories during this time. Time restricted eating allows the body to repair and you can start with a shorter fasting time and gradually increase it.

You can further benefit your health by eating low carbohydrate foods. This can improve your blood sugar and reduce your waistline as blood sugar rises every time you eat, especially with rapidly absorbed sugars and starchy carbohydrates. It subsequently falls, when the quick effect of the rapidly absorbed food wears off. It causes peaks and troughs in the blood sugar resulting in hunger, fatigue and cravings for more sugar. To prevent huge swings in your blood sugar it is best to avoid starchy carbohydrates, sugar and alcohol.

The benefits of calorie restriction and intermittent fasting extend beyond weight loss, and it is suitable for most people who are overweight. However, check with your doctor or health care professional that it is safe for you to do so before you begin.

Fasting is not suitable for the elderly, convalescing, children, during pregnancy or breastfeeding, or if you suffer from or have a history of an eating disorder or have a low BMI or have other medical conditions. Always seek your doctor's advice and especially regarding medication changes.

Getting Started

Depending on how much weight you have to lose and how quickly you wish to shed extra pounds you can decide which weight loss approach to take.

You can:

1. **Restrict yourself to 800 calories a day for 2 weeks and up to a maximum of 12 weeks.**

2. **Follow the 5:2 diet, restricting yourself to 800 calories for 2 days a week and eating sensibly for 5 days.**

3. **Combine fasting and/or non-fasting days with time restricted eating. This means all food should be eaten in an 8–12 hour window each day.**

Plan which days you are fasting so you can be prepared. Increase your fluid intake on these days. Not only will it replace your usual food intake it will help your body eliminate fat. Drinking 2-3 litres a day is advisable.

You can eat your daily calorie limit over 2 or 3 meals, depending on what suits you. Some prefer to extend their overnight fasting by having a late breakfast and early evening meal. However, you can spread your calorie intake over breakfast, lunch and dinner, opting for lighter meals.

You can choose to stick to 800 calories a day for 14 days, or however long you decide, depending on how rapidly you want to lose weight and then switch to the 5:2 diet.

The vegetarian recipes are all calorie counted and listed according to their calorie content. This will make it easy to select what to have for each meal. You can choose whether to have 2 or 3 meals a day. The recipes can be used for whichever meal you choose – just stay within the 800 calorie total on fasting days.

This cookbook also contains recipes for healthy, low-carb, low-calorie desserts, however only eat these in moderation and avoid them completely if you have sugar cravings. These can be reduced or eliminated completely by avoiding sugar and starchy carbohydrates.

Diet Tips

- Staying busy will help take your mind of food, especially when you first start. Get up and do something. Exercise helps, even if it's going for a walk.

- Keep a food diary. Writing down what you eat helps you track your calorie consumption and you can also log how you are feeling including energy, sleep, weight loss and fluid intake. It's great to reflect and see how you're doing.

- Decide when the best time to fast is. Avoiding social get-togethers, holidays and weekends will help you kick start your plan.

- On non-fasting days, don't binge and don't over-do the portions.

- Avoid refined carbohydrates and sugars.

- You can fill up on high volume foods like broccoli, cauliflower, carrots and heaps of lettuce or spinach without adding large amounts of calories.

- At mealtimes, replace starchy carbohydrates with lots of veggies and you'll feel less sluggish and hungry.

- Schedule in easy meals, plan in advance so you avoid temptation. That way you can also avoid missing a meal.

- Drink plenty of water!

- You may experience headaches in the first couple of days as your body adjusts. Relax and drink water. Remember, you need extra fluid as your body burns off fat.

- Prepare some tasty meals and snacks for the fridge or freezer and plan ahead so you aren't tempted to overdo the calories.

- Finding a diet buddy is not only good for morale but you can also swap ideas, recipes and provide encouragement.

- Experiment. You're bound to find your own staples which are handy and quick to prepare.

BREAKFAST, LUNCH & DINNER

Vegetarian
Recipes Under
100 Calories

Carrot & Apple Smoothie

Ingredients

1 medium carrot, peeled

1 apple, cored

¼ cucumber

SERVES 1

78 calories per serving

Method

Place all the ingredients into a blender and add around a cup of water. Blitz until smooth. You can add a little extra water if it's too thick.

Creamy Red Pepper Soup

Ingredients

2 red peppers (bell peppers), de-seeded and finely chopped

2 tablespoons light crème fraîche

600mls (1 pint) hot vegetable stock (broth)

Sea salt

Freshly ground black pepper

SERVES 2

76 calories per serving

Method

Place the red peppers (bell peppers) into a saucepan and pour in the hot stock (broth). Bring the ingredients to the boil, reduce the heat and simmer for a few minutes until the peppers have softened. Using a hand blender or food processor blitz the soup until smooth. Stir in the crème fraîche and season with salt and pepper. Serve and enjoy.

Tomato & Basil Soup

Ingredients

2 x 400g (14oz) tins of chopped tomatoes

1 onion, peeled and chopped

1 small handful of fresh basil, chopped

600mls (1 pint) vegetable stock (broth)

1 tablespoon olive oil

Sea salt

Freshly ground black pepper

SERVES 4

90 calories per serving

Method

Heat the oil in a saucepan, add the onion and cook for 5 minutes until the onion has softened. Add the tomatoes and stock (broth) and bring it to the boil. Reduce the heat and simmer for 5 minutes. Using a food processor and or hand blender blitz until smooth. Add in the basil. Season with salt and pepper. Serve and enjoy.

Creamy Tomato & Pesto Soup

Ingredients

6 large tomatoes

2 stalks of celery, chopped

2 teaspoons pesto

1 tablespoon crème fraîche

600mls (1 pint) hot stock (broth)

Freshly ground black pepper

SERVES 2

84 calories per serving

Method

Place the tomatoes, celery and pesto into a saucepan and add the stock (broth). Cook for 8-10 minutes. Using a hand blender or food processor, blitz the soup until it's smooth. Add the crème fraîche and stir well. Season with salt and pepper then serve. .

Garlic Mushroom Wraps

Ingredients

- 400g (14oz) mushroom, chopped
- 8 Romaine lettuce leaves
- 2 cloves of garlic, chopped
- 2 tablespoons light crème fraîche
- 2 teaspoons olive oil
- ½ teaspoon mustard
- 2 teaspoons soy sauce
- Sea salt
- Freshly ground black pepper

SERVES 2

99 calories per serving

Method

Heat the oil in a frying pan, add the mushrooms, garlic, mustard and soy sauce and cook for around 5 minutes or until the mushrooms have softened. Stir in the crème fraîche and warm it thoroughly. Season with salt and pepper. Spoon some of the mixture into each of the lettuce leaves and eat straight away.

Rosemary & Garlic Kale Chips

Ingredients

250g (9oz) kale leaves, chopped into approx. 4cm (2inch pieces)

2 sprigs of rosemary

2 cloves of garlic

2 tablespoons olive oil

Sea salt

Freshly ground black pepper

SERVES 6

55 calories per serving

Method

Gently warm the olive oil, rosemary and garlic over a low heat for 10 minutes. Remove it from the heat and set aside to cool. Take the rosemary and garlic out of the oil and discard them. Toss the kale leaves in the oil making sure they are well coated. Spread the kale leaves onto 2 baking sheets and bake them in the oven at 170C/325F for 15 minutes, until crispy.

Cauliflower 'Rice'

Ingredients

1 head of cauliflower, approx. 700g (1½ lb)

1 tablespoon olive oil

Sea salt

Freshly ground black pepper

SERVES
4

81
calories
per serving

Method

Place the cauliflower into a food processor and chop until fine, similar to rice. Heat the olive oil in a frying pan, stir in the cauliflower and cook for 5-6 minutes or until softened. Season with salt and pepper. Serve as a tasty alternative to rice.

Vegetarian Recipes Under 200 Calories

Pink Grapefruit & Carrot Smoothie

Ingredients

1 apple, cored
½ pink grapefruit
1 carrot, peeled

SERVES 1

137
calories
per serving

Method

Place all the ingredients into a blender with enough water to cover them and blitz until smooth.

Summer Berry Smoothie

Ingredients

50g (2oz) blueberries
50g (2oz) strawberries
25g (1oz) blackcurrants
25g (1oz) red grapes
1 carrot, peeled
1 orange, peeled
Juice of 1 lime

SERVES 1

146
calories
per serving

Method

Place all of the ingredients into a blender and cover them with water. Blitz until smooth. You can also add some crushed ice or a mint leaf to garnish.

Creamy Strawberry & Cherry Smoothie

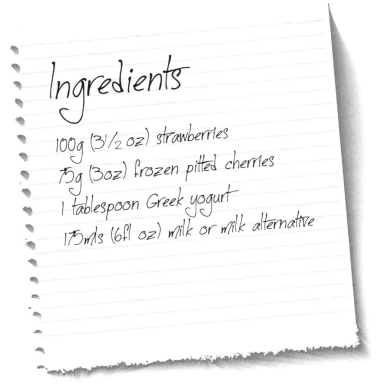

Ingredients

100g (3½ oz) strawberries

75g (3oz) frozen pitted cherries

1 tablespoon Greek yogurt

175mls (6fl oz) milk or milk alternative

SERVES 1

172 calories per serving

Method

Place all of the ingredients into a blender and process until smooth.

Carrot & Ginger Smoothie

Ingredients

1 carrot, peeled
1 banana, peeled
2 cm (1 inch) chunk fresh ginger root, peeled
Juice of 1 lime

SERVES 1

114
calories
per serving

Method

Place the ingredients into a blender with just enough water to cover them and blitz until smooth.

Homemade Hummus & Celery

Ingredients

8 sticks of celery, cut into batons

175g (6oz) tinned chickpeas (garbanzo beans), drained

2 cloves of garlic, crushed

1 tablespoon fresh parsley, chopped

1 tablespoon tahini (sesame seed paste)

Juice of 1 lemon

1 tablespoon olive oil

SERVES 4

112 calories per serving

Method

Place the chickpeas (garbanzo beans) into a blender along with the garlic, tahini and lemon juice. Process until it's smooth and creamy. Transfer the mixture to a serving bowl. Make a small well in the centre of the dip and pour in the olive oil. Sprinkle with parsley. Serve the celery sticks on a plate alongside the hummus.

Carrot, Coriander & Butterbean Soup

Ingredients

400g (14oz) butter beans

4 carrots, chopped

1 onion, chopped

1 courgette (zucchini), chopped

1 clove of garlic, chopped

900mls (1½ pints) vegetable stock (broth)

1 handful of fresh coriander (cilantro), chopped

Sea salt

Freshly ground black pepper

SERVES 4

159 calories per serving

Method

Heat the vegetable stock (broth) in a large saucepan. Add in all of the vegetables except the coriander and butterbeans. Bring them to the boil, reduce the heat and simmer for 20 minutes. Add the butterbeans and stir until warmed through. Add in half of the chopped coriander (cilantro). Using a hand blender or food processor, process the soup until smooth. Sprinkle with the remaining coriander and serve.

Cream Of Mushroom Soup

Ingredients

450g (1lb) mushrooms, chopped

1 large leek, finely chopped

1 tablespoon cornflour (corn starch)

750mls (1½ pints) vegetable stock (broth)

4 tablespoons crème fraîche

1 tablespoon olive oil

Sea salt

Freshly ground black pepper

SERVES 4

120 calories per serving

Method

Heat the olive oil in a saucepan. Add the leek and mushrooms and cook for 8 minutes or until the vegetables are soft. Sprinkle in the cornflour (corn starch) and stir. Pour in the stock (broth), bring it to the boil, cover and simmer for 20 minutes. Stir in the crème fraîche. Using a hand blender or food processor, blend the soup until smooth. Return to the heat if necessary. Season with salt and pepper just before serving.

Avocado & Coriander (Cilantro) Soup

Ingredients

2 avocados

900mls (1½ pints) vegetable stock (broth)

150mls (5fl oz) crème fraîche

2 tablespoons of coriander (cilantro), chopped

Juice of ½ lime

Sea salt

Freshly ground black pepper

SERVES 4

191 calories per serving

Method

Cut the avocados in half, remove and discard the stone then scoop out the flesh. Place the avocado flesh into a blender. Add 4 tablespoons of the crème fraîche and blitz until smooth. In a saucepan, heat the stock (broth) and add the remaining crème fraîche. Add the lime juice to the avocado mixture and mix. Gently stir in the avocado mixture to the vegetable stock, keeping it on a low heat until it's combined. Add the coriander (cilantro). Season and serve.

Asparagus Soup

Ingredients

900g (2lbs) asparagus spears, tough end of stalk removed

2 tablespoons crème fraîche

1 onion, chopped

1 tablespoon olive oil

900mls (1½ pints) vegetable stock (broth)

Sea salt

Freshly ground black pepper

SERVES 4

139 calories per serving

Method

Heat the oil in a large saucepan, add the onion and cook for 5 minutes. Roughly chop the asparagus spears. Place them in the saucepan and add the stock (broth). Bring it to the boil, reduce the heat and simmer for 20 minutes. Use a food processor or hand blender, to process the soup until smooth and creamy. Stir in the crème fraîche. Season and serve.

Slow Cooked Tomato & Butterbean Soup

Ingredients

400g (14oz) tinned tomatoes

400g (14oz) butterbeans

175g (6oz) quinoa, rinsed well

1 onion, peeled and chopped

3 cloves garlic, crushed

1/2 teaspoon dried basil

1/2 teaspoon dried oregano

1/2 teaspoon dried thyme

1 bay leaf

1 small handful of fresh parsley, chopped

750mls (1¼ pints) vegetable stock (broth)

Sea salt

Freshly ground black pepper

SERVES 4

171 calories per serving

Method

Place the tomatoes, quinoa, onion, butterbeans, garlic and herbs into a slow cooker. Pour in the vegetable stock (broth) and still well. Season with salt and pepper. Cook on low for 7 hours or on high for 3 hours. Sprinkle in the parsley before serving.

Mozzarella Slices

Ingredients

300g (11oz) mozzarella cheese, grated (shredded)

4 eggs, beaten

3 cloves of garlic, crushed

2 teaspoons dried oregano

1 cauliflower (approx. 700g), grated (shredded)

Sea salt

Freshly ground black pepper

SERVES 8

157 calories per serving

Method

Place the cauliflower into a steamer and cook for 5 minutes. Place the cauliflower in a bowl and combine it with the mozzarella, eggs, oregano and garlic. Season with salt and pepper. Grease 2 baking sheets. Divide the mixture in half and place it on the baking sheet and press it into a flat rectangular shape. Preheat the oven to 220C/440F. Transfer the baking sheets to the oven and cook for for 20-25 minutes until golden. Slice and serve.

Tomato & Olive Salad

Ingredients

150g (5oz) cherry tomatoes, halved

75g (3oz) black olives, chopped

50g (2oz) capers

1 romaine lettuce, chopped

1 cucumber chopped

1 red pepper (bell pepper), sliced

1 onion, sliced

2 tablespoons red wine vinegar

1 tablespoon freshly squeezed lemon juice

1/2 teaspoon dried oregano

1/2 teaspoon dried basil

3 tablespoons olive oil

Sea salt

Freshly ground black pepper

SERVES 4

176 calories per serving

Method

Pour the vinegar into a large bowl and add in the olive oil, lemon juice, basil and oregano and mix well. Season with salt and pepper. Add the tomatoes, olives, capers, lettuce, cucumber, red pepper (bell pepper) and onion. Toss the salad ingredients in the dressing.

Mediterranean Fried 'Rice'

Ingredients

200g (7oz) mushrooms, finely chopped

6 spring onions (scallions), finely chopped

1 head of cauliflower, approx. 700g (1½lb) broken into florets

1 red pepper (bell pepper), peeled and finely chopped

1 onion, finely chopped

1 large egg, beaten

2 tablespoons olive oil

2 tablespoons soy sauce

Sea salt

Freshly ground black pepper

SERVES 4

149 calories per serving

Method

Place the cauliflower pieces into a food processor and chop until it becomes grain-like. In a bowl mix together the egg with a tablespoon of soy sauce. Heat a tablespoon of oil in a large frying pan or wok. Add the egg mixture and scramble it for a few minutes then remove it and set aside. Heat the remaining olive oil and add in the onion and cook for 5 minutes. Add in all the remaining vegetables and cook them for around 5 minutes until they soften. Stir in the remaining soy sauce. Add the cooked egg mixture and stir well. Season with salt and pepper. Serve instead of traditional fried rice.

Baked Eggs & Peppers

Ingredients

4 eggs
1 red pepper (bell pepper), chopped
1 green pepper (bell pepper), chopped
1 large aubergine (eggplant, chopped
1 bulb of fennel, chopped
1 onion, chopped
3 cloves of garlic, chopped
1 handful of fresh basil
2 tablespoons olive oil

SERVES 4

174
calories
per serving

Method

Place all the vegetables, garlic and basil in a large ovenproof dish. Pour in the olive oil and toss the vegetables. Transfer it to the oven and cook at 200C/400F for 20 minutes. Make 4 round indentations in the vegetables and crack an egg into each space. Place the dish back into the oven and cook for 10 minutes. Serve and eat immediately.

Poached Eggs & Rocket (Arugula)

Ingredients

2 large eggs

25g (1oz) fresh rocket leaves (arugula leaves)

1 teaspoon olive oil

Sea salt

Freshly ground black pepper

SERVES 1

178
calories
per serving

Method

Scatter the rocket (arugula) leaves onto a plate and drizzle the olive oil over it. Bring a shallow pan of water to the boil, add in the eggs and cook until the whites become firm. Serve the eggs on top of the rocket (arugula) and season with salt and pepper.

Cheesy Baked Eggs

Ingredients

4 large eggs

75g (3oz) cheese, grated

25g (1oz) fresh rocket leaves, finely chopped

1 tablespoon parsley

½ teaspoon ground turmeric

1 tablespoon olive oil

SERVES 4

175 calories per serving

Method

Grease each ramekin dish with a little olive oil. Divide the rocket between the ramekin dishes then break an egg into each one. Sprinkle a little turmeric into each one then sprinkle on the cheese. Place the ramekins in a preheated oven at 220C/425F for 15 minutes, until the eggs are set and the cheese is bubbling.

Roast Courgettes & Olives

Ingredients

10 pitted black olives, chopped

4 medium courgettes (zucchinis), thickly sliced lengthways

2 tablespoons tomato purée (paste)

1 clove of garlic, crushed

1 teaspoon mixed herbs

2 tablespoons olive oil

Sea salt

Freshly ground black pepper

SERVES 4

107 calories per serving

Method

In a bowl, combine the olive oil, garlic, tomato purée (paste) and mixed herbs. Place the courgette (zucchini) slices in an ovenproof dish and spread the oil mixture over the slices. Sprinkle with olives and season with salt and pepper. Transfer them to an oven, preheated to 200C/400F and cook for 15 minutes.

Mushroom Courgetti

Ingredients

- 4 courgettes (zucchinis)
- 10 oyster mushrooms, sliced
- 1 red onion, sliced
- 2 tablespoons olive oil
- 2 tablespoons pesto
- 50g (2oz) rocket (arugula) leaves

SERVES 4

165 calories per serving

Method

Spiralize the courgettes into spaghetti. If you don't have a spiralizer, finely cut the vegetables lengthways into long 'spaghetti' strips. Heat the olive oil in a frying pan, add the mushrooms and onions and cook for 2 minutes. Add in the courgettes and the pesto and cook for 5 minutes. Scatter the rocket (arugula) leaves onto plates and serve the courgette on top.

Slow Cooked Citrus Squash

Ingredients

3 onions, finely sliced

2 cloves of garlic

2 butternut squash, peeled and chopped

2 teaspoons ground ginger

1 red chilli, finely chopped

1 small handful of fresh coriander (cilantro), chopped

200mls (7 fl oz) vegetable stock (broth)

2 tablespoons sesame oil

Juice of 2 large oranges

Juice of 2 limes

Sea salt

Freshly ground black pepper

SERVES 4

199 calories per serving

Method

Place all of the ingredients, except the coriander (cilantro) into a slow cooker and stir them wel Cook on low for 4 hours. Season with salt and pepper. Stir in the fresh coriander (cilantro) just before serving.

Roast Pepper & Feta Salad

Ingredients

- 75g (3oz) feta cheese, crumbled
- 2 red peppers (bell pepper), halved and de-seeded
- 2 green peppers (bell peppers), halved and de-seeded
- 2 tablespoons olive oil
- Sea salt
- Freshly ground black pepper

SERVES 4

138 calories per serving

Method

Place the peppers under a hot grill (broiler) until the skins begins to blacken. Remove them and place them inside a plastic bag for several minutes to help loosen the skin. Peel off skin and transfer the peppers to a serving plate. Drizzle with olive oil and sprinkle with feta cheese. Season with salt and pepper.

Slow Cooked Autumn Vegetable Casserole

Ingredients

- 150g (5oz) cherry tomatoes, halved
- 150g (5oz) button mushrooms
- 125g (4oz) soya beans
- 125g (2oz) peas
- 3 cloves of garlic, peeled and chopped
- 2 carrots, peeled and roughly chopped
- 1 whole beetroot, washed and roughly chopped
- 1 butternut squash, peeled and cut into chunks
- 1 medium broccoli, broken into florets
- 1 teaspoon dried thyme
- 1 teaspoon dried oregano
- 1 tablespoon olive oil
- Sea salt
- Freshly ground black pepper

SERVES 4

192 calories per serving

Method

Place all of the ingredients, except the tomatoes, into a slow cooker and mix them well. Cook on low for 3 hours. Add the tomatoes to the slow cooker and continue cooking for 30 minutes. Season with salt and pepper.

Pizza Kale Chips

Ingredients

250g (9oz) kale, chopped into approx.4cm (2 inch) pieces

50g (2oz) ground almonds

50g (2oz) Parmesan cheese

3 tablespoons tomato purée (tomato paste)

1/2 teaspoon mixed herbs

1/2 teaspoon oregano

1/2 teaspoon onion powder

2 tablespoons olive oil

100mls (3 1/2 fl oz) water

SERVES 6

149
calories
per serving

Method

Place all of the ingredients, except the kale, into food processor and process until finely chopped into a smooth consistency. Toss the kale leaves in the mixture. Spread the kale out onto 2 baking sheets. Bake in the oven at 170C/325F for 15 minutes, until crispy.

Mozzarella Chicory Boats

Ingredients

200g (7oz) mozzarella cheese, sliced

200g (7oz) chicory leaves

2 tablespoon fresh basil, chopped

1 tablespoon olive oil

SERVES 4

165 calories per serving

Method

Place the chicory leaves onto a baking sheet. Drizzle them with olive oil then place the cheese on the leaves. Place them under a hot grill (broiler) for around 4 minutes until the cheese has melted. Sprinkle with chopped basil and serve straight away.

Cannellini Stuffed Peppers

Ingredients

400g (14oz) tin of cannellini beans, drained

4 large mushrooms, chopped

3 cloves of garlic, chopped

2 red peppers (bell peppers), top removed and de-seeded

2 yellow peppers (bell peppers), top removed and de-seeded

1 onion, peeled and finely chopped

2 eggs

1 teaspoon paprika

A handful of fresh basil

Sea salt

Freshly ground black pepper

SERVES 4

183 calories per serving

Method

Place the beans, mushrooms, eggs, garlic, onion, basil and paprika into a bowl and mix well. Season with salt and pepper. Scoop some of the mixture into each of the peppers and place the lid back onto the peppers. Place the peppers onto a baking tray. Transfer them to the oven at 180C/ 360F for 20-25 minutes. Serve and eat straight away.

Pomegranate Guacamole

Ingredients

Flesh of 2 ripe avocados
½ onion, finely chopped
Seeds from 1 pomegranate
1 bird's-eye chilli pepper, finely chopped
Juice of 1 lime

SERVES 4

181 calories per serving

Method

Place the avocado, onion, chill and lime juice into a blender and process until smooth. Stir in the pomegranate seeds. Chill before serving. Serve as a dip for chopped vegetables.

Vegetarian Recipes Under 300 Calories

Pineapple & Avocado Smoothie

280
calories
per serving

Ingredients

100g (3½ oz) fresh pineapple, peeled and chopped

1 avocado, peeled & de-stoned

Juice of ½ lemon

Method

Place all of the ingredients into a blender and add enough water to cover them. Process until creamy and smooth.

Raspberry Yogurt Smoothie

Ingredients

50g (2oz) Greek yogurt

125g (4oz) raspberries

½ avocado, stone removed and peeled

Juice of ½ lime

SERVES 1

217
calories
per serving

Method

Toss all of the ingredients into a blender. Blitz until creamy. If it seems too thick you can add some water. Pour and enjoy!

Quinoa & Berry Porridge

Ingredients

75g (3oz) quinoa, cooked

50g (2oz) raspberries

50g (2oz) blueberries

250mls (8fl oz) semi-skimmed milk

Sprinkling of cinnamon

SERVES 1

231 calories per serving

Method

Place the quinoa and almond milk in a saucepan. Bring to the boil and cook for 5 minutes. Sprinkle in the cinnamon. Serve into a bowl, topped off with blueberries and raspberries.

Apple Soufflé Omelette

Ingredients

2 eggs

1 large sweet apple, peeled, cored and chopped

1 teaspoon butter

Sprinkling of cinnamon

SERVES 1

261 calories per serving

Method

Heat the apple with 2-3 tablespoons of water, until it becomes soft and pulpy. Stir in the cinnamon and set it aside. Separate the egg yolks from the whites and whisk the whites into soft peaks. Beat the yolks then fold them into the mixture. Heat the butter in a small frying pan and pour in the eggs. Cook the omelette until the eggs have set but are light and fluffy. Transfer to a plate, spoon on the apple and fold it over. Enjoy.

Easy Banana Pancakes

Ingredients

2 eggs

1 banana, mashed

2 teaspoons olive oil

**SERVES
1**

297
calories
per serving

Method

Whisk the eggs in a bowl and stir in the mashed banana. Combine them until the mixture is smooth. Heat the olive oil in a frying pan, add the pancake mixture and cook for around 2 minutes on each side or until the batter has set and the pancakes are golden. Serve and eat immediately. You can even add a little butter and a sprinkling of cinnamon on top.

Fresh Herb Scramble

Ingredients

2 eggs, whisked

25g (1oz) spinach leaves

1 teaspoon chives, chopped

1 teaspoon fresh basil, chopped

1 teaspoon fresh parsley, chopped

1 tablespoon olive oil

SERVES 1

257 calories per serving

Method

Heat the oil in a frying pan, add the spinach to the pan and cook for 2 minutes. Combine the herbs with the eggs, pour into the pan and stir the mixture until it's lightly scrambled. Season and serve.

Mozzarella & Tomato Mug Omelette

Ingredients

SERVES 1

221 calories per serving

25g (1oz) mozzarella cheese

2 cherry tomatoes, chopped

2 eggs

2 teaspoons chopped red pepper (bell pepper)

1/4 teaspoon dried oregano

1/2 teaspoon softened butter

Method

Crack the eggs into a large mug and beat them. Add in the remaining ingredients. Place the mug in a microwave and cook on full power for 30 seconds. Stir and return it to the microwave for another 30 seconds, stir and cook for another 30-60 seconds or until the egg is set. Alternatively, try plain eggs as a quick and easy alternative to scrambling.

Herby Goat's Cheese Mug Omelette

Ingredients

25g (1oz) goats cheese, crumbled

2 eggs

1/2 teaspoon softened butter (optional)

2 teaspoons fresh basil, chopped

SERVES 1

280
calories
per serving

Method

Whisk the eggs in a large mug. Add in the cheese, basil and butter. Place the mug in a microwave and cook on full power for 30 seconds. Stir and return it to the microwave for another 30 seconds, stir and cook for another 30-60 seconds or until the egg is completely set. Enjoy straight from the mug.

Tomato & Basil Eggs

Ingredients

400g (14oz) tinned chopped tomatoes

4 large eggs, beaten

1 small handful of fresh basil leaves, chopped

1 tablespoon olive oil

Sea salt

Freshly ground black pepper

SERVES 2

252 calories per serving

Method

Heat the olive oil in a pan and add in the chopped tomatoes. Cook for around 10 minutes to reduce the tomato mixture down until the excess juice has evaporated. Slowly pour in the beaten egg, stirring constantly until the egg is completely cooked. Season and sprinkle with basil before serving.

Cheese & Tomato Mini Cauliflower Pizzas

Ingredients

350g (12 oz) mozzarella cheese, grated (shredded)

200g (7oz) passata/ tomato sauce

2 eggs

1 head of cauliflower approx. 700g (1½lb), grated (shredded)

1 teaspoon dried oregano

1 teaspoon dried basil

1 teaspoon garlic powder

1 tomato, sliced

Handful of fresh basil leaves, chopped

SERVES 4

219 calories per serving

Method

Steam the grated (shredded) cauliflower for 5 minutes then allow it to cool. Place the cooked cauliflower in a bowl and add the eggs, half the cheese, all of the dried herbs and garlic and mix everything together really well. Grease two baking sheets. Divide the mixture into 12 and roll it into balls. Place them on a baking sheet and press them down until they are flat and round like mini pizza bases. Transfer them to the oven and bake at 220C/440F for 12 minutes until they are lightly golden. Top each pizza base with a little passata, the remaining mozzarella and tomato and fresh basil. Place the pizzas under a grill (broiler) and cook for 4-5 minutes or until the cheese has melted. Enjoy.

Mediterranean Vegetable Bake

Ingredients

400g (14oz) cannellini beans

150g (5oz) cherry tomatoes, halved

150g (5oz) button mushrooms

3 cloves of garlic, peeled and chopped

3 medium carrots, peeled and roughly chopped

1 large onion, peeled and chopped

1 butternut squash, peeled and cut into chunks

3 celery stalks, chopped

1 courgette (zucchini), chopped

1 teaspoon dried thyme

1 teaspoon dried oregano

1 large handful of fresh basil

A small handful of fresh parsley, chopped

2 tablespoons olive oil

Sea salt

Freshly ground black pepper

SERVES 4

295 calories per serving

Method

Place the beans and vegetables into a roasting tin. Sprinkle in the dried herbs, garlic and olive oil and toss all of the ingredients together. Season with salt and pepper. Transfer them to an oven, preheated to 180C/360F and cook for 30-40 minutes or until all of the vegetables are softened. Scatter in the fresh herbs just before serving.

Bean & Quinoa Casserole

Ingredients

450g (1lb) black-eyed beans, drained
200g (7oz) frozen peas
100g (3½ oz) fresh spinach leaves
100g (3½ oz) quinoa
2 x 400g (14oz) tins of chopped tomatoes
2 cloves garlic, chopped
1 red onion, chopped
1 teaspoon cumin
1 teaspoon dried oregano
½ teaspoon chilli powder
125mls (4fl oz) water
1 tablespoon olive oil

SERVES 4

292 calories per serving

Method

Heat the oil in a saucepan, add the onion and garlic and cook for 5 minutes. Transfer to an ovenproof dish. Add in the quinoa, tomatoes, cumin, oregano and chilli powder. Place the dish in the oven and cook at 180C/360F for 20 minutes. Stir in the beans, peas and water. Cover with foil and cook for 20 minutes. Remove it from the oven, stir in the spinach and allow it to wilt for a couple of minutes before serving.

Courgette Fritters

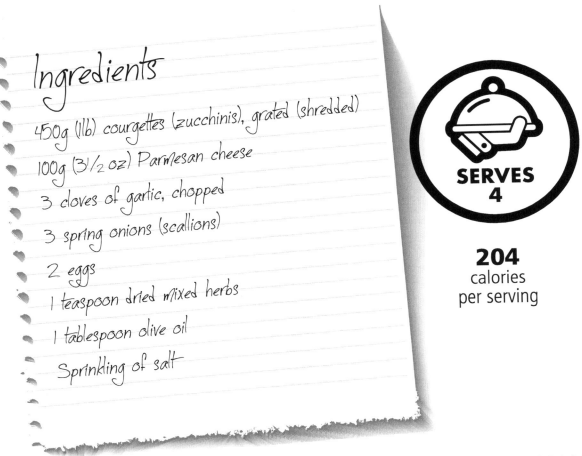

Ingredients

450g (1lb) courgettes (zucchinis), grated (shredded)

100g (3½ oz) Parmesan cheese

3 cloves of garlic, chopped

3 spring onions (scallions)

2 eggs

1 teaspoon dried mixed herbs

1 tablespoon olive oil

Sprinkling of salt

SERVES 4

204 calories per serving

Method

Place the grated (shredded) courgette (zucchini) into a colander and sprinkle with a little salt. Allow it to sit for 30 minutes then squeeze out any excess moisture. Place the eggs, Parmesan, spring onions (scallions), garlic and dried herbs into a bowl and mix well with the courgettes. Scoop out a spoonful of the mixture and shape it into patties. Repeat for the remaining mixture. Heat the oil in a frying pan, add the patties and cook for 2 minutes, turn them over and cook for another 2 minutes. Serve warm.

Aubergine Fries

Ingredients

- 125g (4oz) ground almonds (almond meal/almond flour)
- 1 large egg
- 1 large aubergine (eggplant, cut lengthwise into batons
- 1/2 teaspoon salt
- 1/2 teaspoon ground cumin
- 1/2 teaspoon paprika
- 1 tablespoon olive oil
- Sea salt
- Freshly ground black pepper

**SERVES
4**

255
calories
per serving

Method

Place the ground almonds on a large plate and season with salt and pepper. In a bowl, beat the egg and stir in the cumin, paprika and oil. Dip the aubergine batons in egg mixture then roll them in the almond mixture. Place the aubergine on a baking sheet. Transfer it to the oven and cook at 220C/425F for 15 minutes.

Egg & Lentil Salad

Ingredients

200g (7oz) Puy lentils

4 eggs

4 tomatoes, deseeded and chopped

4 spring onions (scallions), finely chopped

2 tablespoons olive oil

2 tablespoons basil

2 large handfuls of washed spinach leaves

1 clove of garlic

Juice and rind of 1 lemon

Sea salt

Freshly ground black pepper

SERVES 4

231 calories per serving

Method

Place the lentils in a saucepan, cover them with water and bring them to the boil. Reduce the heat and cook for 20-25 minutes. Drain them once they are soft. Heat the olive oil in a saucepan, add the garlic and spring onions (scallions) and cook for 2 minutes. Stir in the tomatoes, lemon juice and rind. Cook for 2 minutes. Stir in the lentils and keep warm. In a pan of gently simmering water, poach the eggs until they are set but soft in the middle which should be 3-4 minutes. Scatter the spinach leaves onto plates, serve the lentils and top off with a poached egg. Season with salt and pepper. Sprinkle with basil and serve.

Mixed Bean Salad

Ingredients

100g (3½ oz) tinned mixed beans, drained

1 hard-boiled egg, quartered

1 medium tomato, chopped

1 spring onion (scallion), finely chopped

2 teaspoons olive oil

1 small handful of fresh basil, chopped

1 large handful of fresh spinach

1 clove of garlic, finely chopped

Zest and juice of 1 lime

Sea salt

Freshly ground black pepper

SERVES 1

266 calories per serving

Method

Heat the oil in a frying pan, add the garlic and spring onions (scallions) and cook for 2 minutes. Stir in the mixed beans, tomato, lime zest and juice. Cook for 3 minutes until the tomatoes are warmed. Stir in the fresh basil and season with salt and pepper. Scatter the spinach leaves onto a plate and serve the lentil mixture on top. Lay the egg on top. Serve and eat straight away.

Mozzarella Roast Vegetables

Ingredients

- 25g (1oz) mozzarella cheese, grated (shredded)
- 4 florets of broccoli, roughly chopped
- 1 small courgette (zucchini), chopped
- 1 red pepper (bell pepper), chopped
- 1 medium tomato, chopped
- 1/2 onion, peeled and roughly chopped
- 1/2 teaspoon mixed herbs
- 1 teaspoon olive oil

SERVES 1

209 calories per serving

Method

Place all of the ingredients, apart from the mozzarella, into a large ovenproof dish and mix them well. Place the vegetables in the oven and cook them at 200C/400F for 20 minutes. Remove the dish from the oven and sprinkle over the mozzarella cheese. Return it to the oven and continue cooking for 5-10 minutes when the cheese is completely melted.

Halloumi & Asparagus Salad

Ingredients

450g (1lb) asparagus

250g (9oz) halloumi cheese, cut into slices

2 large handfuls of spinach leaves

1 tablespoon olive oil

Sea salt

Freshly ground black pepper

SERVES 4

257
calories
per serving

Method

Heat the olive oil in a frying pan and cook the asparagus for 4 minutes or until tender. Remove, set aside and keep warm. Place the halloumi in the frying pan and cook for 2 minutes on each side until golden. Serve the spinach leaves onto plates and add the asparagus and halloumi slices. Season with salt and pepper.

Vegetable & Chickpea Casserole

SERVES 4

252
calories
per serving

Ingredients

- 1 x 400g (14oz) tin of chickpeas (garbanzo beans)
- 1 x 400g (14oz) tin of chopped tomatoes
- 1 medium aubergine (eggplant), thickly chopped
- 2 large courgettes (zucchinis), thickly chopped
- 4 cloves of garlic, chopped
- 2 sweet potatoes, peeled and chopped

- 1 onion, peeled and chopped
- 2 teaspoons ground coriander (cilantro)
- 1 red pepper (bell pepper), deseeded and chopped
- 1 green pepper (bell pepper, deseeded and chopped
- 1 bunch of fresh basil, chopped
- Sea salt
- Freshly ground black pepper

Method

Place all of the ingredients, except for the fresh basil, into a slow cooker and stir well. Cook on low for 6 hours. Season with salt and pepper. Sprinkle in the basil and mix well. Serve on it's own or as a side dish.

Lentil & Sweet Potato Soup

Ingredients

450g (1lb) sweet potatoes, peeled and diced

200g (7oz) red lentils

4 tomatoes, skinned, de-seeded & chopped

1 carrot, chopped

1 onion, chopped

1 red pepper (bell pepper), chopped

1 clove garlic, chopped

1 tablespoon olive oil

2 tablespoons fresh basil, chopped

1 litre (1½ pints) stock (broth)

SERVES 2

229 calories per serving

Method

Heat the olive oil in a saucepan, add the onion and garlic and cook for 4 minutes. Add in the sweet potatoes, carrots, lentils, tomatoes and red pepper (bell pepper) then pour in the stock (broth). Bring to the boil, reduce the heat and simmer for 30 minutes or until the vegetables are soft. Allow to cool for 10 minutes then using a hand blender or food processor blend slightly but leave the soup chunky. Add in the fresh basil leaves and heat further if required before serving.

Tomato & Fennel Gratin

Ingredients

175g (6oz) mozzarella cheese, grated (shredded)

2 x 400g (2 x 14oz) tinned chopped tomatoes

450g (1lb) fennel bulbs, thinly sliced

2 cloves of garlic, chopped

1 onion, peeled and chopped

1 teaspoon dried mixed herbs

2 tablespoons olive oil

1 teaspoon honey

SERVES 4

249
calories
per serving

Method

Preheat the oven to 180C/360F. Scatter the fennel, garlic and onion into a roasting tin and drizzle in the oil. Toss the ingredients well. Transfer it to the oven and cook for 20 minutes. In a bowl, mix together the tomatoes with a teaspoon of honey and the dried mixed herbs. Pour the tomatoes into the roasting tin and return it to the oven for 40 minutes. Scatter the mozzarella over the bake and cook it in the oven for around 5 minutes or until the cheese begins to bubble.

Courgette 'Spaghetti' Pesto & Avocado Dressing

Ingredients

1 medium courgette (zucchini)

½ ripe avocado, peeled and stone removed

1 teaspoon pesto sauce

1 teaspoon olive oil

1 teaspoon lemon juice

SERVES 1

231 calories per serving

Method

Use a spiraliser or if you don't have one, use a vegetable peeler and cut the courgette (zucchini) into thin strips. Heat a teaspoon of oil in a frying pan, add the courgette (zucchini) and cook for 4-5 minutes or until it has softened. In the meantime, place the avocado, pesto and lemon juice and a teaspoon of olive oil into a blender and process until smooth. Add the avocado mixture to the courgette (zucchini) and stir it well. Serve and eat straight away.

Avocado & Orange Salad

Ingredients

2 avocados, peeled and stone removed

3 oranges, peeled

2 teaspoons cardamom pods

Large handful of watercress

2 tablespoons olive oil

½ teaspoon ground allspice

Juice of ½ lime

SERVES 4

250 calories per serving

Method

Cut the orange flesh from the outer skin to remove the individual segments and place them in a bowl. Slice the avocados and add them to the orange segments. Using the back of a spoon or a mortar and pestle, break the cardamom pods open and remove the tiny seeds. In a bowl, mix together the cardamom seeds with the lime juice, olive oil and allspice. Toss the oranges, avocados and watercress in the dressing then serve.

Greek Salad

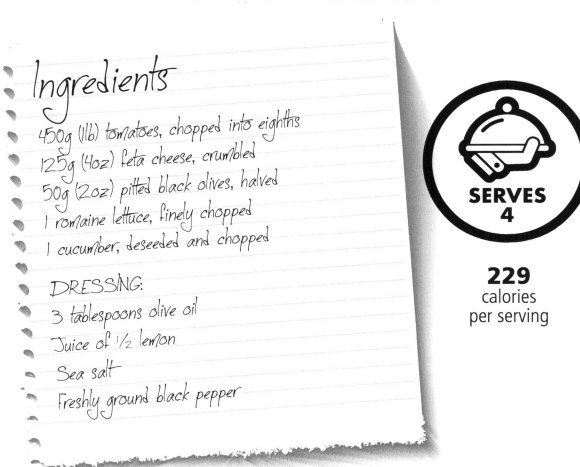

Ingredients

450g (1lb) tomatoes, chopped into eighths

125g (4oz) feta cheese, crumbled

50g (2oz) pitted black olives, halved

1 romaine lettuce, finely chopped

1 cucumber, deseeded and chopped

DRESSING:

3 tablespoons olive oil

Juice of ½ lemon

Sea salt

Freshly ground black pepper

**SERVES
4**

229
calories
per serving

Method

Place all the salad ingredients into a bowl. In a separate bowl, mix together the ingredients for the dressing. Pour the dressing into the salad and toss it well before serving.

Vegetarian Recipes Under 400 Calories

Creamy Lime & Mint Smoothie

Ingredients

250mls (8fl oz) coconut water

8 fresh mint leaves

1 medium avocado, stone and skin removed

Juice of ½ lime

SERVES 1

323 calories per serving

Method

Place the ingredients into a blender and blitz until smooth.

Olive, Tomato & Herb Frittata

Ingredients

50g (2oz) mozzarella cheese, grated (shredded)

75g (3oz) pitted black olives, halved

8 cherry tomatoes, halved

4 large eggs

1 small handful of fresh parsley, chopped

1 small handful of fresh basil leaves, chopped

1 tablespoon olive oil

SERVES 2

343 calories per serving

Method

Break the eggs into a bowl and whisk them then add in the parsley, basil, olives and tomatoes. Add in the cheese and stir it. Heat the oil in a small frying pan and pour in the egg mixture. Cook until the egg mixture completely sets. Place the frittata under a hot grill for 3 minutes to finish it off. Carefully remove it from the pan. Cut into slices and serve.

Avocado & Cheese Omelette

Ingredients

25g (1oz) cheese, grated (shredded)

2 eggs, beaten

Flesh of ½ avocado, chopped

1 teaspoon fresh basil

1 teaspoon olive oil

Freshly ground black pepper

SERVES 1

396
calories
per serving

Method

Heat the olive oil in a frying pan then pour in the beaten egg. When it begins to set, sprinkle on the grated cheese, basil and chopped avocado. Cook until the eggs are completely set and the cheese has melted. Season with black pepper. Serve and enjoy.

Chilli Mushroom & Bean Omelette

Ingredients

50g (2oz) tinned cannellini beans, drained

50g (2oz) mushrooms, chopped

2 eggs

1 red pepper (bell pepper)

1 tablespoon olive oil

Dash of Tabasco sauce or a sprinkle of chilli powder

SERVES 1

341 calories per serving

Method

Heat the olive oil in a pan. Add the mushrooms, pepper (bell pepper) and beans. Cook for 3-4 minutes until the vegetables have softened. Remove them and set aside. Whisk the eggs in a bowl and pour them into the pan. Once the eggs begin to set, return the mushrooms, peppers and beans and spread them onto the eggs. Sprinkle with chilli or Tabasco sauce. Serve and eat straight away.

Cheese & Courgette Omelette

Ingredients

25g (1oz) feta cheese, crumbled

2 eggs

1 small courgette (zucchini), grated (shredded)

1 teaspoon fresh parsley, chopped

1 tablespoon olive oil

SERVES 1

337 calories per serving

Method

Place the eggs in a bowl and whisk them. Stir in the cheese and courgette (zucchini). Heat the olive oil in a frying pan. Pour in the egg mixture and cook until it is set. Sprinkle with parsley and serve.

Halloumi Skewers

Ingredients

400g (14oz) halloumi cheese, cut into thick chunks

4 cloves of garlic, finely chopped

1 teaspoon dried oregano

1 red pepper (bell pepper) cut into 2cm (1 inch) chunks

1 yellow pepper (bell pepper) cut into 2cm (1 inch) chunks

1 onion, peeled and cut into 2cm (1 inch) chunks

1 tablespoon olive oil

2 tablespoons soy sauce

Juice of ½ lime

SERVES 4

385
calories
per serving

Method

Place the olive oil, soy sauce, lime, oregano and garlic into a large bowl and mix well. Add in the halloumi, bell peppers and onion to the bowl. Toss the ingredients in the oil mixture. Cover and refrigerate for at least 1 hour. Thread the halloumi, onion and peppers onto skewers. Place the skewers under a hot grill (broiler). Cook for 5-7 minutes on each side until the chicken is completely cooked through.

Low Carb Vegetable Lasagne

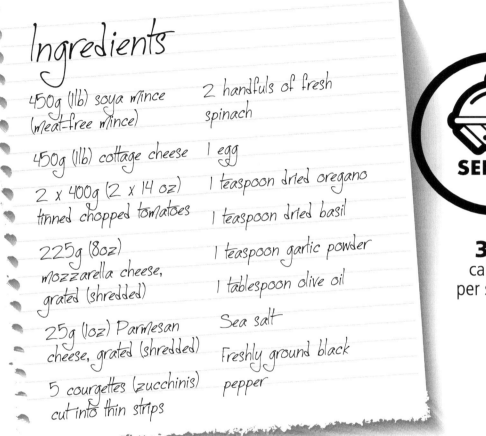

Ingredients

450g (1lb) soya mince (meat-free mince)

450g (1lb) cottage cheese

2 x 400g (2 x 14 oz) tinned chopped tomatoes

225g (8oz) mozzarella cheese, grated (shredded)

25g (1oz) Parmesan cheese, grated (shredded)

5 courgettes (zucchinis) cut into thin strips

2 handfuls of fresh spinach

1 egg

1 teaspoon dried oregano

1 teaspoon dried basil

1 teaspoon garlic powder

1 tablespoon olive oil

Sea salt

Freshly ground black pepper

SERVES 6

343 calories per serving

Method

Lay the courgette (zucchini) slices onto kitchen roll and sprinkle with salt. Set aside for 15 minutes then squeeze it between the sheets of kitchen roll to remove any excess moisture. Heat the oil in a large pan, add the soya mince, herbs and garlic. Cook for 5 minutes, then add the tomatoes and spinach. Bring it to the boil then remove it from the heat. Season with salt and pepper. In a bowl, combine the cottage cheese and egg. Preheat the oven to 180C/360F. Spoon some of the tomato mixture into the bottom of an ovenproof dish. Place a layer of courgette strips on top. Spoon a layer of the tomato mixture on top followed by a layer of cottage cheese. Repeat for the remaining mixture. Finish with a layer of courgette on top, then sprinkle the mozzarella and Parmesan cheese over it. Cover it with foil. Transfer it to the oven and cook for 40 minutes. Remove the foil, return to the oven and cook it for another 15 minutes. Serve with lots of fresh green salad.

Avocado & Black-Eyed Pea Salad

Ingredients

400g (14 oz) black-eyed peas, drained

2 avocados, halved with stone removed

1 red pepper (bell pepper), finely chopped

1 garlic clove, minced

1 teaspoon chopped coriander (cilantro), finely chopped

½ teaspoon ground paprika

1 tablespoon olive oil

Juice of 1 lime

Sea salt

Freshly ground black pepper

SERVES 4

311 calories per serving

Method

To make the dressing, put the lime juice in a large bowl and whisk in the olive oil. Stir in the black eyed peas, red pepper (bell pepper), coriander (cilantro), garlic, paprika, salt and black pepper. Mix together until everything is coated with the dressing. Place the avocado halves on 4 plates. Spoon the mixture over the avocado and serve.

Vegetarian Breakfast Casserole

Ingredients

200g (7oz) button mushrooms

100g (3½ oz) cheese, grated (shredded)

12 eggs

4 tomatoes, roughly chopped

3 carrots, peeled and grated (shredded)

2 handfuls of fresh spinach

2 potatoes, peeled and diced (you could use leftovers too)

1 red pepper (bell pepper), deseeded and chopped

1 teaspoon sea salt

400mls (14fl oz) milk (or milk alternative)

1 tablespoon olive oil

Freshly ground black pepper

SERVES 6

328 calories per serving

Method

Preheat the oven to 190C/380F. Heat the oil in a frying pan. Add the carrots, potatoes, red pepper (bell pepper) and mushrooms and cook for around 7 minutes, until they have softened. Add in the spinach and tomatoes and cook for 2 more minutes. Transfer the ingredients to an ovenproof dish. In a bowl, whisk together the milk and eggs. Season with salt and pepper. Pour the egg into the vegetables. Sprinkle the cheese over the top. Transfer it to the oven and cook for 40-45 minutes, or until golden.

Feta & Spinach Slice

Ingredients

225g (8oz) feta cheese, grated (shredded)

125g (4oz) ground almonds

25g (1oz) fresh spinach leaves, chopped

2 eggs

1 onion, finely chopped

1 teaspoon baking powder

200mls (7fl oz) almond milk

SERVES 4

378 calories per serving

Method

Place the spinach into a saucepan, cover it with warm water, bring it to the boil and cook for 3 minutes. Drain it and set aside. Place the ground almonds in a bowl and add in the eggs, milk and baking powder and mix well. Add in the chopped onion, spinach and feta and combine the mixture. Spoon the mixture into a small ovenproof dish and smooth it out. Transfer it to the oven and bake at 190C/375F for 35 minutes. Cut into slices before serving.

Herby Tomato, Cannellini & Feta Salad

Ingredients

400g (14oz) tinned cannellini beans, drained
250g (9oz) cherry tomatoes, halved
75g (3oz) feta cheese, crumbled or diced
50g (2oz) fresh rocket (arugula) leaves
2 tablespoons fresh basil leaves, chopped
1 tablespoon fresh parsley, chopped
2 tablespoons olive oil
Juice of ½ lemon
Sea salt
Freshly ground black pepper

SERVES 2

364
calories
per serving

Method

Place all of the ingredients into a bowl and mix well. Season with salt and pepper. Chill before serving.

Mozzarella & Aubergine Rolls

Ingredients

125g (4oz) mozzarella cheese, grated (shredded)

2 tomatoes, chopped

6 asparagus spears

1 aubergine (eggplant), cut into 6 length-ways slices

1 tablespoon fresh basil, chopped

1 tablespoon fresh chives, chopped

2 tablespoons olive oil

SERVES 2

336 calories per serving

Method

Heat the olive oil in a frying pan, add in the aubergine (eggplant) slices and cook for 2-3 minutes on each side. In the meantime, steam the asparagus for 5 minutes until it has softened. Place the aubergine slices onto plates and sprinkle some cheese, tomatoes and herbs onto each slice. Add an asparagus spear. Roll the aubergine slices up and secure it with a cocktail stick. Serve and enjoy.

Italian Lentil Salad

Ingredients

450g (1lb) green lentils

100g (3½ oz) hazelnuts, chopped

2 spring onions (scallions), chopped

1 cucumber, peeled and diced

1 red pepper (bell pepper), sliced

1 handful of fresh basil

Zest and juice of 1 lemon

100mls (3½ fl oz) olive oil

Sea salt

Freshly ground black pepper

SERVES 4

362 calories per serving

Method

Cook the lentils according to the instructions then allow them to cool. Pour the olive oil and lemon juice into a jug and combine them. Season with salt and pepper. Place all the ingredients for the salad into a bowl and pour on the olive oil and lemon juice.

Avocado & Beetroot Salad

Ingredients

3 small cooked beetroots, sliced

1 small avocado, stone removed, peeled and sliced

1 handful of fresh spinach leaves

2 teaspoons olive oil

½ teaspoon paprika

1 teaspoon lemon juice

Sea salt

Freshly ground black pepper

SERVES 1

341 calories per serving

Method

Scatter the spinach leaves on to a plate. Lay the slices of beetroot and avocado on top of the leaves. In a small bowl, mix together the oil, paprika and lemon juice. Season with salt and pepper. Pour the oil dressing over the salad. Enjoy straight away.

Greek Style Salad

Ingredients

350g (12oz) tomatoes, chopped
150g (5oz) feta cheese, crumbled
50g (2oz) pitted black olives, chopped
1 small onion, peeled and chopped
1 iceberg lettuce, finely chopped
1 cucumber, de-seeded and chopped

DRESSING:
3 tablespoons olive oil
Juice of 1 lemon
Sea salt
Freshly ground black pepper

SERVES 4

371
calories
each

Method

In a bowl, mix together the dressing ingredients. Place all of the salad ingredients into a bowl and add in the dressing. Toss the salad well before serving.

Tomato, Feta & Pomegranate Bake

Ingredients

- 450g (1lb) cherry tomatoes, halved
- 75g (3oz) pomegranate seeds
- 2 blocks of feta cheese, halved widthways
- 2 teaspoons ground coriander
- 1/2 teaspoon chilli powder
- 1 tablespoon olive oil
- 1 handful of fresh parsley, chopped

SERVES 4

328 calories per serving

Method

Scatter the tomatoes into an oven proof dish, and sprinkle with coriander (cilantro) and chilli powder. Transfer it to the oven and cook at 220C/440F for 15 minutes. Lay the feta on top of the tomato mixture, drizzle with the olive oil. Return it to the oven and continue cooking for 7-10 minutes or until the feta is golden. Sprinkle with the pomegranate seeds and parsley. Serve with a heap of green salad.

Halloumi & Vegetable Traybake

Ingredients

- 350g (1lb) halloumi cheese, thickly sliced
- 25g (1oz) pine nuts
- 8 cherry tomatoes, halved
- 3 cloves of garlic, chopped
- 1 yellow pepper (bell pepper), deseeded and chopped
- 1 red pepper (bell pepper), deseeded and chopped
- 2 onions, peeled and chopped
- 1 handful of fresh basil, chopped
- 1 handful of fresh parsley, chopped
- 1 tablespoon olive oil
- 2 teaspoons paprika

SERVES 4

378 calories per serving

Method

Preheat the oven to 200C/400F. Scatter the tomatoes, onions, peppers and garlic into a roasting tin. Coat them in paprika and olive oil. Toss them well in the mixture. Lay the halloumi on top of the vegetables. Transfer it to the oven and cook for 25 minutes or until the halloumi is golden. Add in the parsley, basil and pine nuts and serve.

Roast Balsamic Vegetables

Ingredients

4 tomatoes, chopped

2 red onions, chopped

3 sweet potatoes, peeled and chopped

100g (3oz) red chicory (or if unavailable use yellow)

300g (8oz) potatoes, peeled and chopped

5 stalks of celery, chopped

1 bird's-eye chilli, de-seeded and finely chopped

100g (3½ oz) kale, finely chopped

2 tablespoons fresh parsley, chopped

2 tablespoons fresh coriander (cilantro) chopped

3 tablespoons olive oil

2 tablespoons balsamic vinegar

1 teaspoon mustard

SERVES 4

300 calories per serving

Method

Place the olive oil, balsamic, mustard, parsley and coriander into a bowl and mix well. Toss the remaining ingredients into the dressing and season with salt and pepper. Transfer the vegetables to an ovenproof dish and cook in the oven at 200C/400F for 45 minutes.

Smokey Bean & Mushroom Stew

Ingredients

- 400g (14oz) black-eyed peas
- 400g (14oz) haricot beans
- 400g (14oz) tinned tomatoes, chopped
- 225g (8oz) mushrooms, sliced
- 150g (5oz) sweetcorn
- 2 garlic cloves, chopped
- 2 onions, chopped
- 1 tablespoon smoked paprika
- 1 red chilli, finely chopped
- 1 large handful of parsley
- 250mls (8fl oz) vegetable stock (broth)
- 1 tablespoon soy sauce (low sodium)
- 1 tablespoon olive oil

SERVES 4

354 calories per serving

Method

Heat the oil in a saucepan, add the onions and garlic and cook for 4 minutes until the onions have softened. Stir in the mushrooms, chilli, haricot beans, black-eyed peas, tomatoes, sweetcorn, paprika and soy sauce and cook for 5 minutes. Pour in the stock (broth) and simmer for 15 minutes. Stir in the parsley and serve into bowls.

Spicy Bean Bake

Ingredients

- 2 x 400g (2 x 14oz) tins of chopped tomatoes
- 400g (14oz) tin of black beans, drained and rinsed
- 175g (6oz) cheese, grated (shredded)
- 175g (6oz) quinoa
- 125g (4oz) sweetcorn
- 2 cloves of garlic, finely chopped
- 1 tablespoon olive oil
- 1 onion, finely chopped
- 1 green pepper (bell pepper), deseeded and finely chopped
- 1 courgette (zucchini), diced
- ½ teaspoon ground cumin
- 1 teaspoon oregano
- 1 teaspoon paprika
- 1 teaspoon chili powder
- Juice of ½ lime
- 400mls (14fl oz) vegetable stock (broth)

SERVES 6

316 calories per serving

Method

Preheat the oven to 180C/360F. Cook the quinoa according to the instructions and then drain it. Place the onion, peppers, garlic, courgette (zucchini), beans, tomatoes and sweetcorn in a bowl and mix well. Add in the spices, oil and lime juice to the mixture. Scoop it in to an ovenproof dish or roasting tin. Add in the quinoa and mix well. Transfer it to the oven and bake for 40 minutes. Remove the dish from the oven and sprinkle the cheese on top. Return it to the oven and cook for another 5-10 minutes, or until the cheese is bubbling. Serve with a heap of green salad.

Desserts
Under
230 Calories

Raspberry & Pistachio Fool

Ingredients

100g (3½ oz) plain (unflavoured) Greek yogurt

100g (3½ oz) raspberries

10 pistachio nuts, chopped

Zest and juice of ½ a lime

SERVES 2

200 calories per serving

Method

Place the raspberries into a blender and purée until smooth. Place the yogurt, lime zest and jui
into the raspberry puree. Stir but don't mix it completely, aim for a swirled affect. Spoon the
yogurt and raspberry mixture into 2 serving glasses or bowls. Top it with the pistachio nuts an
serve.

Chocolate Truffles

Ingredients

75g (3oz) smooth peanut butter

50g (2oz) desiccated (shredded) coconut

25g (1oz) chia seeds

25g (1oz) coconut oil

2 teaspoons coconut flour

1 tablespoon 100% cocoa powder

1 tablespoon stevia sweetener

Cocoa powder for coating (approx. 1 tablespoon)

MAKES 12

102 calories per ball

Method

Place all the ingredients into a bowl or food processor (apart from the cocoa powder for coating) and process until smooth. Using a teaspoon, scoop out a little of the mixture, shape it into a ball and roll it in cocoa powder. Chill before serving.

Nutty Chocolate Treats

Ingredients

125g (4oz) walnuts, chopped

125g (4oz) almonds, chopped

50g (2oz) coconut oil

50g (2oz) desiccated (shredded) coconut

2 eggs, beaten

2 tablespoons peanut butter

2 tablespoons 100% cocoa powder (or cacao nibs)

2 tablespoons tahini (sesame) paste

1 tablespoon sunflower seeds

1 tablespoon stevia

1 teaspoon ground cinnamon

MAKES 24

128 calories per serving

Method

Place all the ingredients into a bowl or a food processor and mix it well, keeping the nuts a nice chunky texture. Spoon the mixture into small paper baking cases. Transfer them to the oven and bake at 180C/360F for 20 minutes. Allow them to cool then store them in an airtight container.

Berry Compote & Vanilla Yogurt

Ingredients

- 250g (9oz) blueberries
- 250g (9oz) strawberries
- 100g (3½ oz) redcurrants
- 100g (3½ oz) blackberries
- 4 tablespoons plain yogurt
- ½ teaspoon vanilla essence
- Zest and juice of 1 orange

SERVES 4

139 calories per serving

Method

Place all of the berries into a pan along with the orange zest and juice. Gently heat the berries for around 5 minutes until warmed through. Mix the vanilla essence into the yogurt. Serve the berries with a dollop of yogurt on top.

Tropical Skewers & Fruit Sauce

Ingredients

2 bananas, peeled and thickly sliced

1 pineapple, (approx. 2lb weight) peeled and diced

400g (14oz) strawberries

1 teaspoon 100% cocoa powder or cacao nibs

SERVES 4

167 calories per serving

Method

Place the cocoa powder/cacao nibs and 125g (4oz) of strawberries into a food processor and blitz until creamy. Pour the sauce into a serving bowl. Skewer the bananas, pineapple chunks and remaining strawberries onto skewers. Serve the sauce alongside the skewers.

Spiced Poached Pears

Ingredients

4 pears

4 star anise

2 cinnamon sticks

300mls (½ pint) hot water

SERVES 4

68 calories per serving

Method

Place the water, star anise and cinnamon into a saucepan and bring it to the boil. Add the pears, reduce the heat and simmer gently for 10 minutes. Remove them from the water and serve

Raspberry Cupcakes

Ingredients

250g (9oz) ground almonds (almond flour/almond meal)

150g (5oz) fresh raspberries

3 eggs, whisked

1 teaspoon baking powder

1 teaspoon stevia powder (or to taste)

50mls (2fl oz) melted coconut oil

Pinch of salt

MAKES 10

228 calories each

Method

Lightly grease a 10-hole muffin tin. In a bowl, combine the ground almonds (almond flour/almond meal), baking powder, stevia and salt. In another bowl, combine the coconut oil and eggs then pour the mixture into the dry ingredients. Mix well. Add the raspberries to the mixture and gently stir them in. Spoon some of the mixture into each of the muffin moulds. Transfer them to the oven and bake at 170C/325F for around 20 minutes or until golden.

You may also be interested in other titles by
Erin Rose Publishing
which are available in both paperback and ebook.

 Quick Start Guides

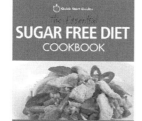

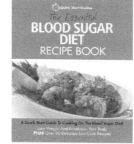

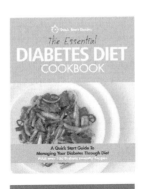

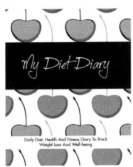

You may also be interested in titles by
Pomegranate Journals

Printed in Great Britain
by Amazon